World Languages
JAPANESE
For Kids

Written & Illustrated
By Sachiko Otohata

We have dedicated considerable time and effort to ensure the accuracy and cultural sensitivity of our content. However, if you find any errors or have suggestions, please feel free to contact us at factorysachi.com. Your input is crucial for us to refine and improve our offerings for young learners.

Copyright © 2025 Sachiko Otohata

All rights reserved. No part of this book may be used or reproduced in any manner whatsoever without written permission except in the case of brief quotations embodied in critical articles and reviews.

While the author has used their best efforts in preparing this book, they make no representations or warranties with respect to the accuracy or completeness of the content.

Writing and illustrations: Sachiko Otohata
Published in Canada

If you enjoyed this book, please consider leaving a review online. As an independent publisher, every review helps more parents and children discover and learn about this book.

◉ factorysachi.com
🌐 factorysachi (Instagram/Facebook/TikTok)

This book was inspired by my child,
to whom I am deeply grateful.

With love to all who wish to pass on
the beauty of Japanese to future generations.

Sachiko Otohata

Don't forget to check out the rest of
the World Languages series.

Fun and educational companion books
for coloring, activities, drawing,
and taking notes!

Hello! My name is Sachiko.
こんにちは！ わたしの なまえは さちこ です。
Konnichiwa! Watashi no namae wa Sachiko desu.

I live in Japan. It is a country full of wonderful foods, friends, and fun activities!
わたしは にほんに すんでいるの。
にほんには おいしい たべもの と
やさしい ともだち と
たのしいこと が たくさんあるよ！

Watashi wa Nihon ni sunde iru no.
Nihon ni wa oishii tabemono to
yasashii tomodachi to
tanoshii koto ga takusan aru yo!

One of the most exciting things in my world is the Japanese language.

わたしの せかいで いちばん わくわくする ことは 「にほんご」です。

Watashi no sekai de ichiban wakuwaku suru koto wa "Nihongo" desu.

Like a little key, each new word you learn opens a door to understanding people and places.

ことばは、ちいさな かぎみたい。ひとつ おぼえる たびに、あたらしい とびらが ひらきます。

Kotoba wa chiisana kagi mitai. Hitotsu oboeru tabi ni, atarashii tobira ga hirakimasu.

Let me guide you into this exciting world!

わたしと いっしょに にほんごの せかいを たんけんしよう！

Watashi to issho ni nihongo no sekai o tanken shiyou!

How to Use This Book:

How to write the word in Japanese letters

Apple ⇌ りんご

Rin-go

How to say the word

Scan the QR code to hear the phrases!

OR

www.factorysachi.com/jpsound

Everyone speaks a little differently! The pronunciation shown in this book is just a helpful guide — you might hear small differences depending on who is speaking.

Thank You ⇋ ありがとう
A-ri-ga-tou

Good Night ⇋ おやすみなさい
O-ya-su-mi-na-s

Sorry ⇋ ごめんなさい
Go-men-na-sai

Please ⇋ おねがいします
O-ne-gai shi-mas

Excuse Me ⇋ すみません
Su-mi-ma-se

Good Morning ⇋ おはよう
O-ha-yoh

Hello ⇋ こんにちは
Kon-ni-chi-wa

Goodbye ⇋ さようなら
Sa-yoh-na-ra

Greetings ⇋ あいさつ
Ai-sa-tsu

Younger Brother ⇆ おとうと　**Younger Sister** ⇆ いもうと
Oh-toh-toh　　　　　　　　　　　　　　Ee-moh-to

Older Sister ⇆ おねえさん　**Older Brother** ⇆ おにいさん
Oh-neh-san　　　　　　　　　　　　　　Oh-nee-sa

Aunt ⇆ おばさん　　　　　**Uncle** ⇆ おじさん
Oh-ba-san　　　　　　　　　　　Oh-ji-san

Baby ⇆ あかちゃん　**Cousin** ⇆ いとこ　**Pet** ⇆ ペッ
Ah-kah-chan　　　　　　　Ee-toh-ko　　　　　Pet-

Grandmother ⇌ おばあさん
Oh-ba-a-san

Grandfather ⇌ おじいさん
Oh-ji-i-san

Father ⇌ おとうさん
Oh-toh-san

Mother ⇌ おかあさん
Oh-kah-san

Who do you live with? ⇌ だれ と すんでる?
Da-re toh sun-de-ru?

Family ⇌ かぞく
Ka-zoh-ku

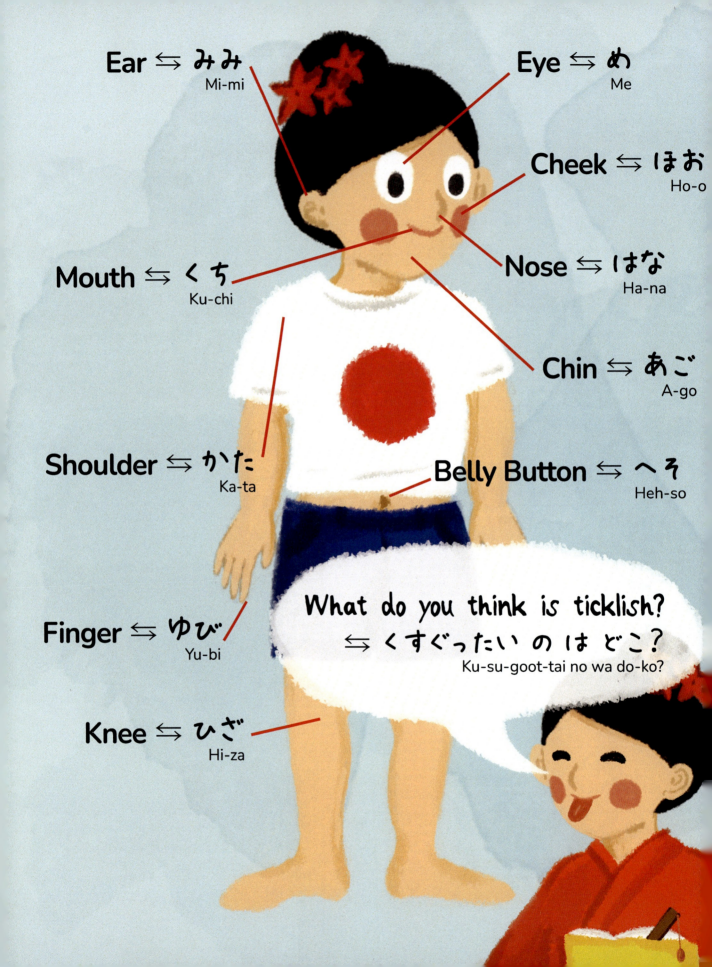

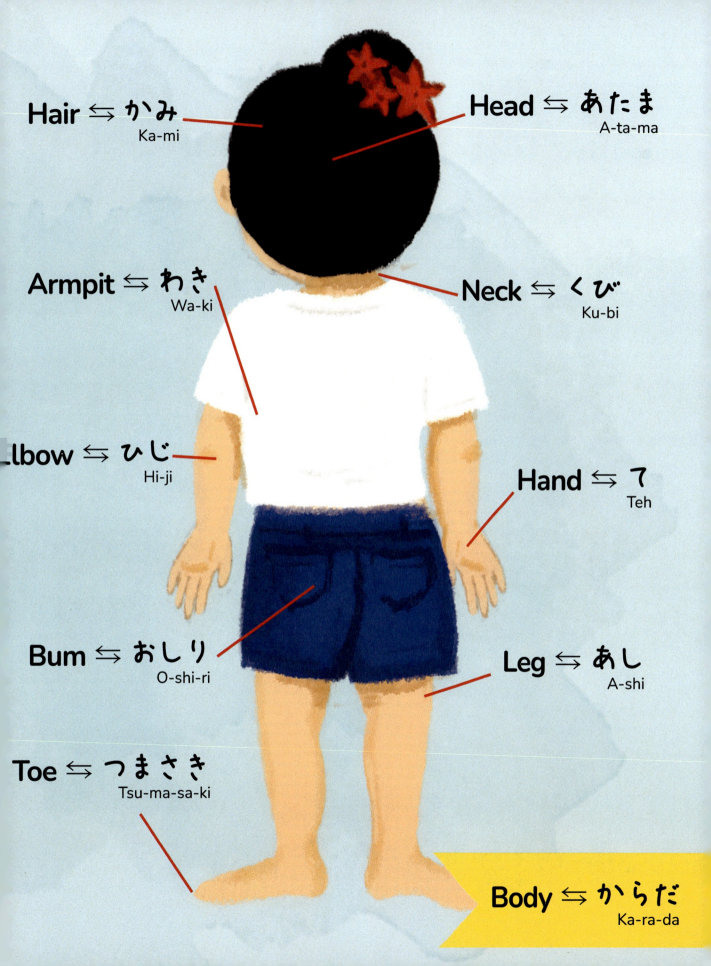

Shirt ⇆ シャツ
Sha-tsu

Dress ⇆ ワンピース
Wan-pi-su

Pajamas ⇆ パジャマ
Pa-ja-m

Skirt ⇆ スカート
Soo-ka-toh

Socks ⇆ くつした
Ku-tsu-shi-ta

Pants ⇆ ズボン
Zu-bo

Shoes ⇆ くつ
Ku-tsu

Hat ⇆ ぼうし
Boh-shi

T-Shirt ⇋ Tシャツ
Tee-sha-tsu

Underwear ⇋ したぎ
Shi-ta-gi

Bag ⇋ かばん
Ka-ban

Scarf ⇋ マフラー
Ma-fu-rah

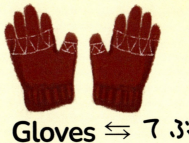
Gloves ⇋ てぶくろ
Teh-bu-ku-ro

What are you wearing?
⇋ なに きてる?
Na-ni ki-te-ru?

Glasses ⇋ めがね
Meh-ga-ne

Clothes ⇋ ふく
Fu-ku

Draw ⇋ えをかく
Eh-oh ka-ku

Sing ⇋ うたう
U-ta-u

Play ⇋ あそぶ
Ah-so-bu

Cook ⇋ りょうりする
Ryo-ri su-ru

Read ⇋ よむ
Yo-mu

Eat ⇋ たべる
Ta-beh-ru

Sleep ⇋ ねる
Ne-ru

Drink ⇋ のむ
No-mu

What do you like to do? ⇋ なに したい？
Na-ni shi-ta-i?

Wash ⇋ あらう
A-ra-u

Things To Do ⇋ すること
Su-ru ko-toh

Bananas ⇆ バナナ
Ba-na-na

Strawberries ⇆ いちご
Ee-chi-go

Apple ⇆ りんご
Rin-go

Grapes ⇆ ぶどう
Boo-doh

Corn ⇆ とうもろこし
To-mo-ro-ko-shi

Carrot ⇆ にんじん
Nin-jin

Mushrooms ⇆ きのこ
Ki-no-ko

Tomato ⇆ トマト
Toh-ma-toh

Onion ⇆ たまねぎ
Ta-ma-neh-gi

Cheese ⇆ チーズ
Chee-zu

Potato ⇆ じゃがいも
Ja-ga-i-mo

Cucumber ⇆ きゅうり
Kyuu-ri

Yogurt ⇆ **ヨーグルト**
Yo-gu-ru-to

Milk ⇆ **ぎゅう にゅう**
Gyu-nyu

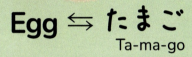
Egg ⇆ **たまご**
Ta-ma-go

Bread ⇆ **パン**
Pan

Candy ⇆ **キャンディー**
Kyan-di

What's do you think is yummy?
⇆ なに が おいしい?
Na-ni ga o-i-shii?

ish ⇆ **さかな**
Sa-ka-na

Rice ⇆ **ごはん**
Go-han

Food ⇆ **たべもの**
Ta-beh-mo-no

Cow ⇌ うし
Oo-shi

Pig ⇌ ぶた
Bu-ta

Chicken ⇌ にわとり
Ni-wa-toh-ri

Squirrel ⇌ りす
Ri-su

Mouse ⇌ ねずみ
Neh-zu-mi

Rabbit ⇌ うさぎ
Oo-sa-gi

Dog ⇌ いぬ
Ee-nu

Bird ⇌ とり
Toh-ri

Horse ⇋ うま
Oo-ma

Sheep ⇋ ひつじ
Hi-tsu-ji

Fox ⇋ きつね
Ki-tsu-neh

Duck ⇋ あひる
A-hi-ru

What's your favorite animal?
⇋ すきな どうぶつ は?
Su-ki-na doh-u-bu-tsu wa?

Cat ⇋ ねこ
Neh-ko

Animals ⇋ どうぶつ
Doh-bu-tsu

Sun ⇄ たいよう
Ta-i-yoh

Sky ⇄ そら
So-ra

Ocean ⇄ うみ
U-mi

What do you think is beautiful?
⇄ なに が きれい?
Na-ni ga ki-re-i?

Flower ⇄ はな
Ha-na

Nature ⇄ しぜん
Shi-zen

Rainy ⇋ **あめ**
A-meh

Cloudy ⇋ **くもり**
Ku-mo-ri

Sunny ⇋ **はれ**
Ha-re

Windy ⇋ **かぜ**
Ka-zeh

Snowy ⇋ **ゆき**
Yu-ki

Rainbow ⇋ **にじ**
Ni-ji

Lightning ⇋ **かみなり**
Ka-mi-na-ri

Spring ⇋ はる
Ha-ru

Summer ⇋ なつ
Na-tsu

Fall ⇋ あき
A-ki

Winter ⇋ ふゆ
Fu-yu

What's the weather like today?
⇋ きょう の てんき は?
Kyo-u no ten-ki wa?

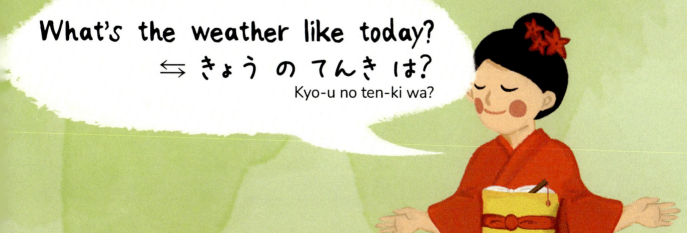

Seasons & Weather ⇋ きせつ と てんき
Ki-se-tsu toh ten-ki

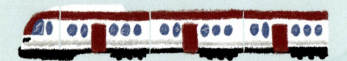

Train ⇆ でんしゃ
Den-sha

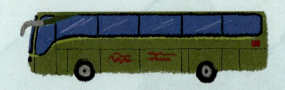

Bus ⇆ バス
Ba-su

Bicycle ⇆ じてんしゃ
Ji-ten-sha

Car ⇆ くるま
Ku-ru-ma

Airplane ⇆ ひこうき
Hi-kou-ki

Fire Truck ⇆ しょうぼうし
Sho-bo-sh

Ambulance ⇆ きゅうきゅうしゃ
Kyuu-kyuu-sha

Truck ⇆ トラック
Toh-rak-ku

Motorcycle ⇆ オートバイ
Oo-toh-ba-i

Police Car ⇆ パトカー
Pa-toh-kaa

Helicopter ⇆ ヘリコプター
Heh-ri-ko-pu-ta

What would you like to ride on?
⇆ なに に のりたい？
Na-ni ni no-ri-ta-i?

Boat ⇆ ふね
Fu-ne

Vehicles ⇆ のりもの
No-ri-mo-no

Park ⇆ **こうえん**
Ko-en

Grocery Store ⇆ **スーパー**
Suu-paa

School ⇆ **がっこう**
Gak-kou

Hospital ⇆ **びょういん**
Byoh-in

Train Station ⇆ **えき**
E-ki

Library ⇆ **としょかん**
Toh-sho-kan

Cafe ⇆ カフェ
Ka-feh

Restaurant ⇆ レストラン
Re-su-toh-ran

Where do you like to go?
⇆ どこ に いきたい?
Do-ko ni i-ki-ta-i?

Town ⇆ まち
Ma-chi

Pencil ⇆ **えんぴつ**
En-pi-tsu

Marker ⇆ **マーカー**
Maa-kaa

Crayon ⇆ **クレヨン**
Ku-re-yon

Book ⇆ **ほん**
Hon

Paper ⇆ **かみ**
Ka-mi

Notebook ⇆ **ノート**
Noh-toh

Water Bottle ⇋ すいとう
Sui-toh

Ball ⇋ ボール
Boh-ru

Glue ⇋ のり
No-ri

Eraser ⇋ けしゴム
Ke-shi-go-mu

What do you take to school?
⇋ がっこう に なに もって いく？
Gak-ko-u ni na-ni moh-te i-ku?

Computer ⇋ コンピューター
Kon-pyuu-ta

School ⇋ がっこう
Gak-koh

Red ⇆ あか
A-ka

Yellow ⇆ きいろ
Kii-ro

Blue ⇆ あお
A-oh

Green ⇆ みどり
Mi-do-ri

White ⇆ しろ
Shi-ro

Black ⇆ くろ
Ku-ro

Brown ⇆ ちゃいろ
Cha-i-ro

Pink ⇆ ピンク
Pin-ku

Orange ⇆ オレンジ
O-ren-ji

Gray ⇆ はいいろ
Hai-i-ro

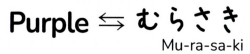

Purple ⇆ むらさき
Mu-ra-sa-ki

What's your favorite color? ⇆ すきな いろ は?
Su-ki-na i-ro wa?

Colors ⇆ いろ
I-ro

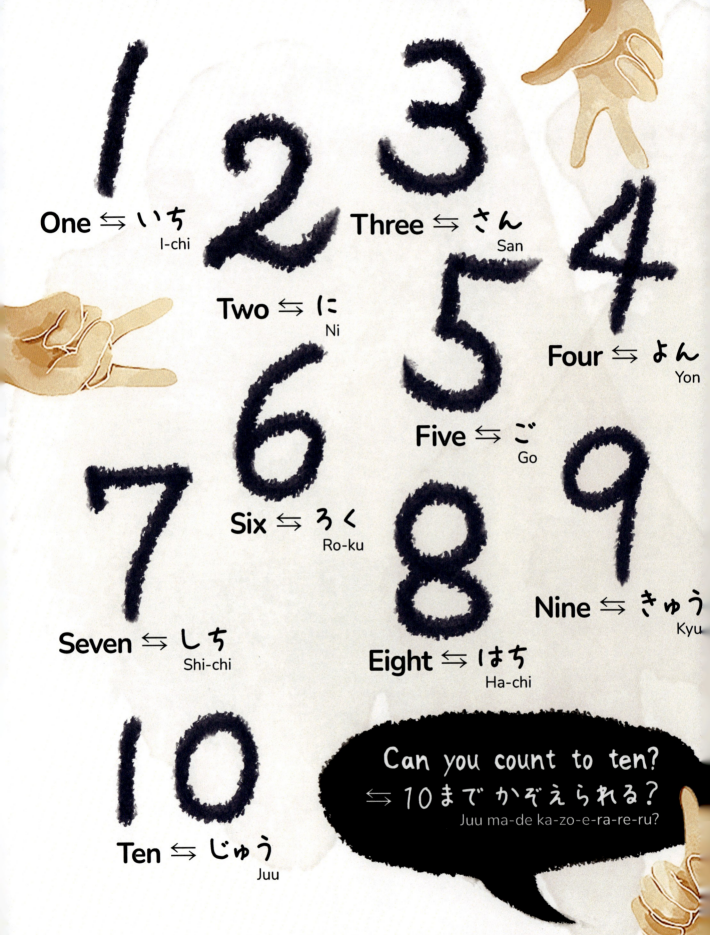

Circle ⇋ まる
Ma-ru

Square ⇋ しかく
Shi-ka-ku

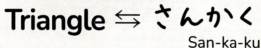
Triangle ⇋ さんかく
San-ka-ku

Heart ⇋ ハート
Haa-toh

Crescent ⇋ みかづき
Mi-ka-zu-ki

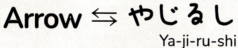
Arrow ⇋ やじるし
Ya-ji-ru-shi

Pentagon ⇋ ごかくけい
go-kah-koo-kay

Rectangle ⇋ ちょうほうけい
Chou-ho-u-kei

Numbers & Shapes ⇋ かず と かたち
Ka-zu toh ka-ta-chi

Grilled Chicken Skewer ⇆ やきとり
Ya-ki-toh-ri

Boxed Lunch ⇆ べんとう
Ben-to

Noodle Soup ⇆ ラーメン
Raa-men

Dried Seaweed ⇆ のり
No-ri

Green Tea ⇆ りょくちゃ
Ryo-ku-cha

Sumo Wrestling ⇆ すもう
Su-moh

Soybean Soup ⇆ みそしる
Mi-so-shi-ru

Sushi ⇆ すし
Su-shi

Fortune Cat ⇆ まねきねこ
Ma-ne-ki ne-ko

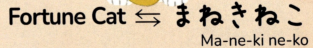

Rice Ball ⇆ おにぎり
O-ni-gi-ri

Fried Shrimp & Vegetables ⇆ てんぷら
Ten-pu

Hot Spring ⇌ おんせん
On-sen

Mount Fuji ⇌ ふじさん
Fu-ji-san

Japanese Traditional Robe ⇌ きもの
Ki-mo-no

Cherry Blossom ⇌ さくら
Sa-ku-ra

Wishing Doll ⇌ だるま
Da-ru-ma

Paper Folding Art ⇌ おりがみ
O-ri-ga-mi

Wooden Doll ⇌ こけし
Ko-ke-shi

What would you like to see? ⇌ どれ を みたい?
Do-re o mi-ta-i?

Things From Japan ⇌ にほんの もの
Ni-hon no mo-no

Good Evening ⇋ こんばんは
Kon-ban-wa

Yes / No ⇋ はい／いいえ
Hai / Ii-

Nice To Meet You ⇋ はじめまして
Ha-ji-me-ma-shi-teh

I'm Home ⇋ ただいま
Tah-dai-ma

I'm Leaving ⇋ いってきま
It-te-ki-r

Thank You For The Meal ⇆ いただきます
I-ta-da-ki-mas

I've Finished Eating ⇆ ごちそうさま
Go-chi-soh-sa-ma

Help! ⇆ たすけて！
Ta-su-ke-teh

I Love You ⇆ すきです
Su-ki des

More Useful Phrases ⇆ もっと つかえる ことば
Moh-toh tsu-kah-eh-ru koh-toh-ba

Toys ⇋ おもちゃ
O-mo-cha

Doll ⇋ にんぎょう
Nin-gyou

Robot ⇋ ロボット
Ro-bot-to

Friend ⇋ ともだち
To-mo-da-chi

Gift ⇋ プレゼント
Pu-re-zen-to

Juice ⇋ ジュース
Juu-su

Ice Cream ⇆ アイスクリーム
Ai-su-krii-mu

Cake ⇆ ケーキ
Kee-ki

Donut ⇆ ドーナツ
Dou-na-tsu

What do you like the best?
⇆ なに が いちばん すき？
Na-ni ga i-chi-ban su-ki?

Chocolate ⇆ チョコレート
Cho-ko-ree-to

Things Kids Love ⇆ こども が すきな もの
Ko-doh-mo ga su-ki na mo-no

Amusement Park ⇆ ゆうえんち
Yuu-en-chi

Pool ⇆ プール
Puu-ru

Birthday ⇆ おたんじょうび
O-tan-jou-bi

Slide ⇆ すべりだい
Su-be-ri-dai

Nap ⇆ ひるね
Hi-ru-ne

Piggyback Ride ⇆ おんぶ
On-bu

Maze ⇆ めいろ
Me-i-ro

Coloring ⇆ ぬりえ
Nu-ri-e

What do you think is fun?
⇆ なに が たのしい?
Na-ni ga ta-no-shi-i?

Swings ⇆ ぶらんこ
Bu-ran-ko

Things Kids Love ⇆ こども が すきな もの
Ko-doh-mo ga su-ki na mo-no

Our journey through Japan is almost over
にほんの たびは そろそろ おしまい。
Nihon no tabi wa sorosoro oshimai.

But the adventure never ends.
でも ぼうけんは ずっと つづきます。
Demo, bōken wa zutto tsuzukimasu!

Thank you for traveling with me!
Keep learning, keep exploring,
and make your world even bigger.

いっしょに たびしてくれて ありがとう！
まなびつづけて、たんけんして、あなたの せかいを
もっと ひろげよう！

Issho ni tabi shite kurete arigatou!
Manabi tsuzukete, tanken shite, anata no sekai o
motto hirogeyou!

The End
おしまい

Oshimai

Made in United States
Orlando, FL
26 August 2025

64307570R00033